MANY A FLOWER

MANY A FLOWER

Ron Dixon

Book Guild Publishing
Sussex, England

First published in Great Britain in 2010 by
The Book Guild Ltd
Pavilion View
19 New Road
Brighton, BN1 1UF

Typesetting in Garamond by
SetSystems Ltd, Saffron Walden, Essex

Printed in Great Britain by
CPI Antony Rowe

A catalogue record for this book is available from
The British Library

ISBN 978 1 84624 429 2

To:
Me Dad

John William (Jack) Dixon

Full many a flower is born to blush unseen
And waste its sweetness on the desert air.

Gray's Elegy

Contents

1 Deadly Nightshade – *Atropa belladonna* 1

2 Sweet Pea – *Lathyrus odoratus* 7

3 Forget-me-Not – *Myosotis sylvatica* 21

4 Melancholy Thistle – *Cirsium heterophyllum* 35

5 Flowering Cherry – *Prunus spp.* 43

6 Baby Blue Eyes – *Nemophila menziesii* 53

7 Poor Man's Orchid – *Schizanthus pinnatus* 59

8 Thrift – *Armeria maritima* 71

9 Bats-in-the-Belfry – *Campanula trachelium* 81

10 Ice Plant – *Sedum spectabile* 87

Photographic Acknowledgements

The author and publisher would like to thank the *Sunderland Echo*, Sunderland City Libary and Arts Centre and the Local Studies Library for permission to reproduce photographs as indicated on the relevant pages. Special thanks are also due to Susan Swinney of the *Sunderland Echo* for her help in providing photographs.

1

Deadly Nightshade

Atropa belladonna

My most vivid memory of the war was of a clear, still autumn night. The full moon shone with a ghostly white daylight effect. People called it a hunter's moon and for me this had a very special meaning because tonight I was the prey. Lying alone in the cold bedroom upstairs, with my head under the coarse grey blanket, I was shivering with fear. Occasionally I peeped out and whispered, "Please God, don't let them come tonight". But I knew they would. They came mostly at night and tonight would be a perfect night for them. Then it happened.

It started with a low whistle which got louder and louder until it developed into an ear-piercing scream. It lasted only a few seconds, but it seemed like an eternity and I was sure this time the bomb would get me. This was followed by an earth-shattering explosion, which told me someone else had been hit. It was quite near, because the house gave a sharp shudder. After a short pause, there was the clattering sound of debris hitting our roof tiles. Meanwhile, I curled up in

1

a tight ball under the bedclothes in case the windows caved in.

The Heinkel bombers had come in low over the sea in order to avoid detection and launch a surprise attack. They entered the estuary of the River Wear only a short distance away from us, looking to drop their load of high explosives on the docks and shipyards in Sunderland. Their other choice targets would be the Monkwearmouth and Alexandra bridges, and damage to them would cut the town in half causing major disruption. A bomb on any of the pitheads would also trap all the miners working on the coalface hundreds of feet below. Thankfully, the bridges and mines escaped major damage for the duration of the war.

The sirens started to wail soon after, telling us all to take cover – as if we needed telling. When the antiaircraft guns started firing, the bombers would turn for home and jettison their excess bombs, usually on the nearby houses. As our house was one of these, we were greatly at risk, so it seemed only a matter of time before we would get hit.

It was in the middle of this pandemonium that we made the short dash to the dug-out shelter in the garden, taking what bedding we could carry for what was going to be a long, cold, damp night on those narrow bunks. A flask of hot tea was prepared in advance every night for this eventuality and it was almost always needed.

A small amount of water lay under the slatted floorboards of the shelter, even though we managed to bail most of it out earlier that day. In prolonged wet weather this was a constant and thankless task as it merely refilled from the surrounding land. Pulling a sacking curtain and board over the narrow doorway to contain the light and deflect any bomb blast, the hurricane lamp was lit and gave out its dim glow with an overpowering smell of paraffin oil. The alternative to the lamp, when paraffin wasn't available, was a tallow candle. These were bright yellow and made from various types of animal fat that had gone rancid and not fit for any other purpose. When lit they gave off a vile malodorous smell, so that darkness was almost preferable. Another feature of these candles was the fact that, when they were blown out, they continued to smoke for some time afterwards with an even worse smell. Lying on those tiered bunks under damp blankets, with condensation running down the corrugated metal walls, sleep was almost impossible. There was also the ever-present thought that the shelters would not withstand a direct hit and there were chilling tales of people buried alive with the waters rising or being trapped with burning paraffin oil. In addition to this, all hell had broken loose outside.

The Stuka dive-bombers had now arrived as always, to try to destroy the anti-aircraft batteries and prepare the way for the next wave of heavy bombers. They were the most terrifying of all because, apart from their renowned accuracy, they were fitted with a fiendish wailing siren that became louder and more highly pitched to become a deafening scream as their speed increased in the dive. The sole purpose of this was to put the fear of God into the gun crews and population below – and very effective they were too. Most of the anti-aircraft batteries were sited fairly near to our houses on the coast. Their main priority was to defend the sensitive targets, so again our houses were in the line of enemy fire and we suffered a barrage of both high explosive and incendiary bombs. Peeping out you could see the flickering lights of burning houses and smell the dense smoke. It was during these night raids that the nearby Blue Bell Hotel was demolished as well as the houses in Sea Road near our school. Perhaps worst of all were the 500kg parachute mines that were designed to explode at roof level to maximise the blast and casualties. One of these fell on Fulwell rail crossing, about three hundred yards from home and, despite the above-ground detonation, made a crater ten feet deep and thirty feet across. Again our house managed to avoid damage but those further away had windows blown in.

Finally, in the early hours of the morning, the blessed monotone of the all-clear would sound and we could crawl outside and try to get some sleep indoors. This of course, was assuming they didn't come again, which happened quite often. Thankfully, the house had managed to escape major damage, although from the sound of nearby shouting and the smell of burning it had been a near miss.

The following day before school, and in spite of dire warnings about unexploded bombs, I would collect the large sharp pieces of steel shrapnel and trophies to compare with classmates at school and tell our own tales of the night's events. The shrapnel was splintered bomb casings and the pieces could be about the size of your hand. The hard shiny steel was about an inch thick and had razor sharp, jagged edges. The effect if being hit by one of these can only be imagined.

I was only seven when the war started and now at nine, apart from those terrifying nights, it was an almost accepted way of life for us in Sunderland. At this time I was living with my sister Madge and husband Tom together with their four-year-old son Derek. Madge was the middle of my three sisters and sixteen years older than me and it was thought, wrongly as it turned out, that it would be safer for me away from the blitzes in the south.

In common with the general population, availability of food was one of our main obsessions. In spite of rationing, supply was variable and much of my free time from school was spent looking for it. Queuing at shops therefore became such a way of life that, if I saw a queue on the way home from school, I would automatically join it and eventually I would ask someone nearby if they knew what it was for – which they frequently didn't!

Bread queues were one of the most common sights and very occasionally, non-rationed fish and chips if there were sufficient supplies. Very rarely, oranges were available, but only on production of a green ration book for a child under five and then only one. Bananas were non-existent and it was not until about two years after the end of the war that I tasted my first one. To allow for a possible queue I was given a half-crown coin (12½p today), under threat of dire unspecified punishment if it wasn't spent wisely. Occasionally, after queuing for some time the air-raid siren would sound, but my place in the line would be far too precious to lose. I have lasting memories of seeing a bomb fall while I crouched down in front of a shop with the other people in case of scattered debris. Worse still would be the flying glass if the blast blew the shop window in.

I have another vivid memory, a recurring nightmare, of being on the Alexandra Bridge in the middle of a bombing raid. I had forgotten the time and been out late with a friend. It was quite dark and when I was walking home across the bridge, the air-raid siren started. My mate had left me to go home because his house was before the bridge. I was totally alone on the deserted bridge, because most people wanted to be at home before nightfall, in case there was a raid. The bridge is about a quarter of a mile long and so there was no quick way of escape. There was an upper disused railway track over the roadway, which now housed anti-aircraft guns and searchlights and made it even more of a prime target. I knew also that the river was a long way below and I had visions of falling into the dark waters with all the steel girders around me if the bridge was hit. As I was running, a bomb fell nearby, because one of the shipyards was almost directly under the bridge. After an eternity, I finally reached the end where it was only relatively safe and I collapsed on the road in a state of almost unconscious breathlessness, thankful that I had been spared – on this occasion at least.

2

Sweet Pea

Lathyrus odorata

Surprisingly enough, during these difficult and dangerous times, all schooling was continued with some semblance of normality. It must be admitted however that 'normality' was a relative term, because our school hours were often interrupted by air raids. The one advantage now however, was that it was difficult for the bombers to make surprise attacks, so daylight raids were less frequent than the night ones. We were therefore given an adequate siren warning to enable us to take cover in the brick-built shelters in the playground. These were also far more comfortable than ours at home and the presence of teachers and classmates gave an added sense of comfort and security. In some respects, it was perhaps a false sense of security, because a hit on a similar shelter nearby killed forty people as the nine-inch thick reinforced concrete roof collapsed on them.

The rate of absenteeism of course was fairly high and many pupils never returned. It was just assumed that the reason lay in the nightly raids, but we never questioned this too closely. Looking back, it's surprising how we took the loss of our classmates in such a matter of fact way. The young seem to have an ability to deal with these emotions in their own way. Friendship bonds are easily made at a young age and just as easily broken, and dwelling too much on their loss may only serve to whip up hysteria.

Our teacher, Mrs Bundy, was generally feared and respected by the whole class, the former mainly due to her frequent use of a stout bamboo cane about three feet long which she used with great effect on our outstretched hands, while we stood in front of the class. The cane was a slightly darker colour than that usually associated with bamboo and quite polished. This was probably caused by age and regular use, but we swore that it had been specially treated to make it more effective. Although by no means obese, Mrs Bundy was a large-framed middle-aged woman, with quite an attractive face when she was in her occasional good moods. The basic punishment for minor transgressions was one stroke, to be doubled if the hand was withdrawn too soon due to fear. Worse than this however would be the lack of respect from fellow classmates. The choice of hand was optional, but you usually offered the left because the other one would have made it impossible to write for at least half an hour afterwards. Occasionally however, some transgressions warranted a stroke on both hands, which made writing a really painful ordeal. Writing anyway wasn't very easy with the crude pens, consisting of a thin wooden dowel for a handle, which held a detachable steel nib. The ink was prepared by dissolving powder in water, which naturally made the nib go rusty after a while. It was also a matter of luck whether you had a good nib, as the quality was very variable, and the standard of writing depended on whether it was new, or had gone rusty. Despite these rather primitive materials a great deal of emphasis was placed on the style of handwriting. All up-strokes had to be thin with thick down-strokes and with a uniform slope to the right. There were even handwriting competitions held between schools and a lot of time was spent copying text just for the exercise.

It has to be admitted on reflection, that we always felt that our punishments were justified and we bore no resentment or thought that they might have been unfair. This is a testimony to our respect for authority, which now seems to be lacking in schools. At the same time, it has to be admitted that we were living in violent times. The cane was particularly feared in winter when our hands were freezing cold, and the lack of circulation prolonged the time before the pain subsided. Although we didn't realise it, her reign of terror probably had its root in her frustration caused by the nightly air raids and lack of attention from Mr. Bundy who had been conscripted into the army. In her defence, it has also to be said that "Owld Vinegar Tits" must have had a particularly difficult job trying to control a group of semi-feral, hyperactive kids who lived with their nerves on a knife-edge. Despite this, she was an excellent teacher who was able to fire the imagination. She always gave encouragement for achievement and her influence will be with me for the rest of my life. When I wasn't in her bad books, I was one of her brightest pupils, possibly because I used books as a kind of refuge from the thoughts of those dreadful nights.

Naturally enough, there were many fanciful treatments designed to relieve the effects of the cane and these were recommended by the frequent offenders, including myself, who were experts in this field. Mickey Murray's was perhaps the most believable and generally adopted. "If yer piss on yer 'ands, it 'ardens the skin and makes 'em numb", he said with an air of authority. I think this was common practice in the coalmines to hasten the healing of blisters on the hands when using pickaxes, but I never could understand the connection between this and the relief of pain. He was also a bit uncertain about the duration of the treatment, so it was assumed that it would be applied frequently over an extended period. The natural consequence of this was that there was always a powerful smell of stale urine in the class. This was not only due to those taking the 'cure' but also due to the fact that many pupils of both sexes suffered from nocturnal incontinence caused by the nightly raids and the effect on their nerves. It was not surprising really, when we walked a daily tightrope between life and oblivion.

Of the other cures, Donny Warton swore by vinegar, while Eric Acheison said he found horse-hair to be effective. I was at a loss to understand either how he obtained or used it, or how it escaped the eagle eye of Mrs Bundy. You didn't want to press him too closely on detail because he was a big lad and it wasn't wise to test his limited powers of logic. I tried to express my doubts on one occasion and was merely told to "Fuck off", which I was pleased to do, as I had got off quite lightly.

It was about this time that I felt the first strong stirrings of awakening sexuality, although there were occasional strange and comforting sensations 'down there' in my earlier years. I was now starting to look at girls differently, and the object of my affection and cause of occasional bouts of priapism was a girl in my class by the name of Joyce Linley. Although never blatantly on show – I was never an exhibitionist – the obvious signs always drew admiring glances from the boys and fits of giggles from the girls. Joyce was a stunning blue-eyed girl with a lovely smile and almost shoulder-length blonde hair, which hung in ringlets. So great was my passion for this young goddess that I was quite oblivious to her shortcomings, the main one being that she suffered from frequent colds, which occasionally caused pale green 'candles' to appear on her upper lip. The common treatment for colds at this time was a piece of camphor tied into a small cloth bag and hung around the neck next to the skin. The reasoning behind this was that the fumes released by the warmth of the body were inhaled and cleared the nasal passages while killing the "germs". The odour made a strange combination when blended with her own incontinence problem, but such is the pulling power of developing hormones, that I became oblivious to this after a short while. Of course it has to be admitted that, in common with most of the class, my own personal hygiene left something to be desired. For her part, she encouraged and returned my affection freely, occasionally rewarding me with a quick tight-lipped kiss when in the presence of her friends. In this way she paraded me as a kind of trophy to boost her standing among them. It also did the same for me as far as the boys were concerned.

As mentioned earlier, the other competing obsession constantly occupying my mind at this time was the need for food. This was hardly surprising when all that physical development which was taking place, coupled with boundless nervous energy, caused a nagging and persistent demand for sustenance. Against this, how-ever, was the fact that food rationing meant that regular meals were something of a luxury and were greedily devoured, although they seldom seemed to satisfy. As a bonus, a regular supply of food was available in the farmers' fields of vegetable crops, and our small group of classmates would often wander far into the countryside after school. After sneaking through a gap in the hedge we would take whatever was available from the nearest crop row. Brushing off the surplus earth on a sleeve, we would hungrily share a raw swede, turnip, potatoes, or carrots to last us until the next meal of, perhaps, baked bean shepherd's pie or dried egg omelette and mash. I'm sure the farmers turned a blind eye to us and, in any case, the loss to their crops was negligible.

The dietary problems of life today have often caused nutritionists to comment that our wartime diet of low fat and protein was one of our healthiest. This may well be true from the point of view of obesity, but in my own case it has had a lasting effect of nervous gastritis and duodenal ulcers. In contrast however, my somewhat unhygienic feeding habits have left me almost immune to minor gastric infections. I also have a legacy of avoiding food waste and a keen interest in cooking, particularly using those recipes making the best use of cheaper ingredients.

Two highlights of the school year occurred every autumn, for which holidays were granted. These were blackberry and "chetty" gleaning weeks. The first, as the name suggests, was an opportunity to top up the diet with freely available fruit from the hedgerows, and the second served the dual purpose of cleaning the fields for the farmers after the potato crop was in. It provided us with some welcome tiny new potatoes which otherwise would sprout up as volunteer weeds in the next year's crop. The tool used for this was called a "howker", a type of short-handled swan-necked hoe, which almost every family had. It was originally used to "howk" small pieces of coal from the slag heaps left by the mines. Later this was made illegal, presumably to prevent trespass, but also for safety reasons, because the tipping buckets were constantly working overhead. Although we worked hard, we still made it enjoyable, with occasional groping in the hedgerows with the girls who 'reluctantly' managed to give us encouragement. At the same time they were quite capable of looking after themselves if too many liberties were taken. My cousin Margaret lived next door and was in the same class as me. On one occasion, I wound her up too far and she rewarded me with a hard kick in the groin, which hurt so much I was unable to stand for nearly an hour afterwards and could only walk bent double after that. It was a silly thing for me to do in the first place, because she was a big lass who far outweighed me. Margaret was aunt Edith's only daughter and rather spoilt, so she was merely told she shouldn't have done it. After some discussion between my sister and aunt, they decided that I needed to be examined by the doctor. I now remember with acute embarrassment lying on his couch, minus trousers and pants, with him groping my bits while the two women were studying and discussing them in detail. Such a traumatic experience could well have had a lasting effect on many a lesser mortal! The doctor charged three shillings and six pence and Aunt Edith agreed to pay half as I was partly to blame.

In the north only a few fruits could be grown, so blackberries were particularly valued, sometimes supplemented with the occasional apple. If someone had an apple with their lunch, they would soon acquire a friend who might get the "gowk" or core. This would all be greedily devoured, except for the pips, which were meticulously removed, because it was generally known that if you swallowed a pip, a tree could grow inside you.

Our packed lunch for school was usually a slice of greyish bread and margarine or lard, sometimes with a light sprinkling of sugar.

Because we were on the coast we were sometimes favoured with a food source not generally available to inland folk. This occurred when the boats came in with a catch of herrings although, unfortunately, it was not a very reliable harvest. The fish were shovelled straight off the boats and piled up onto large open barrows, which the men wheeled around the streets and sold for two pence each. This source of protein was a great treat and was hungrily devoured. Many and varied are the ways of cooking and preserving herring and the fish is still one of my favourites today.

The other great obsession, as with all Geordies, was football and it was both played and followed from a very early age. Whenever there was a home game at Roker Park, almost all the boys in the class would attend. This was the time when the entrance fee for kids was affordable from their meagre pocket money, and our heroes were often locals who had businesses, or at least lived in the town. Alex Hastings, who played centre half, could be seen in his newsagent's shop on the sea front near to our house. Johnny Spuler also had a business in the town and it was great to have a chat with them. To see them on the pitch on Saturday was then even more special. My brother John even had a trial for Sunderland boys but rugby was his main interest. How different it is today, when the cost is generally prohibitive for the very youngsters who should be encouraged.

Every boy in the class loved to play football and in summer the longer days meant there was less likelihood of daylight raids, which allowed us to play after school. The matches took place on a large area of turf behind the promenade and beach and the area was large enough to allow us to play well away from the sea front. This was just as well, because if the ball went over, it would certainly have been lost below on the beautiful sandy beach to which access was prevented by barbed wire. This was because the beach was mined and was to remain so for the duration of the war.

Teams were chosen as a result of lengthy discussions in class time, which often ended with a caning. Of course, we still ran the risk of sporadic bombing raids and on our pitch overlooking the beach we would be the first in the bomber's sights. Strangely, this never crossed our minds as we felt a false sense of security while concentrating on the game within our group of friends.

There was one other source of discomfort, which was a result of wartime conditions. Good quality cloth was virtually unobtainable and the only kind of material available for our school clothes was a coarse wool flannel that felt like sandpaper on the skin. In particular the short trousers worn by the boys chafed the tender skin on the inside of the thighs, to the point where they were permanently red and extremely sore. For some reason it always seemed worse in winter. The common, and only, remedy for this was calamine lotion and although giving instant relief, it had very little lasting effect. By and large, it was a condition we learned to live with, as one does with almost any discomfort.

Winter came early in the north with heavy snowfalls that never seemed to feel too cold. The heavy snow usually meant that overhead power lines would be brought down, but this was merely an inconvenience for people accustomed to damage from the blitzes. In any case, most of our heating, cooking and hot water were adequately supplied by the coal fire and the best candles were used to provide light indoors. By and large, winter was a magical time for us kids. Extraneous sounds seem to be absorbed by the snow and the world took on a dream-like quality of softness and twinkling lights.

Most of us had some ability with wood working, at least as far as sledge construction was concerned. In fact, it was a matter of personal pride to have a sledge at least as good, if not better, than your mates. One group activity for both girls and boys was the cultivation and upkeep of a slide of polished ice in the street. After checking the soles of everyone's boots and shoes, the first one would take a run up and start sliding at a chosen spot followed in quick succession by the others, each one going a little further. Soon a glassy strip of ice would be formed, eventually stretching for twenty to thirty yards. With very little practice and a fast approach you could eventually slide at quite high speeds. When it was too dark to see we reluctantly would have to go indoors. Of course this activity was frowned on and today such a hazard would never be tolerated.

Another item of school clothing almost universally worn was the knitted jumper or "ganzey". They were knitted from oddments of wool that had been rewound from any other items of knitted clothing that had worn out or became holed. I had become quite adept at knitting from a fairly early age and could knit socks and mittens as well as ganzeys, even extending to quite intricate Fair Isle patterns. The design paid no regard to colour or even thickness of the wool, because a new length was simply knotted in when the other one ran out, In fact, one of my ganzeys had half of one arm thicker than the other!

Generally speaking, the standard of education in the

north suffered as a result of wartime conditions and as I showed some promise, Mrs Bundy felt that I was not able to develop my full potential. It could be of course, that this was a diplomatic ploy to try to be rid of a troublesome pupil, but I'm sure her motives were genuine. Consequently, at a meeting with my sister, it was agreed that I would be allowed to try my hand at an Eleven Plus entrance exam from Essex, since I already had connections there. The outcome was that I did rather well and so I was shipped back to Essex to join my father who, prior to his second marriage, was living alone in the family home in Romford.

And so started the next five-year stage of my education in a technical college, which was then the equivalent of a grammar school. The college was the choice of my brother Len, on the grounds that all northeners would automatically become engineers if they were successful. At the time I had to bow to his superior wisdom, but perhaps he was ultimately right.

One event, which I will never forget, occurred when there was an announcement that the beach was finally cleared of mines and the barbed wire would be removed on a given date in March. And so, on a glorious sunny day, I went with Len for our first swim in the sea with our costumes and towels. It was an occasion of great excitement because the golden velvety sand and blue sea had been denied us for so long.

Some of my classmates were already running around on the beach when we arrived and we quickly stripped down to our knitted woollen trunks that we wore under our clothes. The first shock came when we walked down the beach and put a foot into the water.

The intense icy cold hit like a sledgehammer and caused a numbing pain before all feeling was lost. Despite this and because we had waited so long, we cautiously pressed forward and I was fascinated to see that our legs had turned bright blue as I lost feeling there as well. When the first little wave hit my balls and the pain took my breath away, I decided that enough was enough and turned to go back. It was at this moment that a stupid fat lad came tearing down the beach and belly-flopped beside me. With his limited mental powers, he had no idea that the water would be so cold and in any case, he was well protected with a generous layer of blubber. Meanwhile, I was covered with his spray and fell over from the shock, losing the will to live. Len managed to drag me out and I dressed with great difficulty due to the uncontrollable shivering. It was only after some hours that my body temperature returned to normal and I have since treated the North Sea with great respect, even on warm summer days. The lovely colourful coastline of the northeast is to be admired for its scenic beauty only and should not be used for physical enjoyment except by the most hardy local folk. Even so, it was a common sight to see people "sunbathing" in deck chairs on the beach fully insulated in heavy coats and scarves with the men wearing their cloth caps. Another strange custom was that the stalls on the beach sold hot water for people to make their own warming drinks – but there are many strange customs among us northern folks!

3

Forget-Me-Not

Myosotis sylvatica

I was the youngest of three elder sisters and three brothers, the next oldest being my brother Leo who was eight years older than me. My father lost mum when I was only five shortly after we had moved to Essex. Sadly, there are no photos to remind me of her and my only memory is of an infirm lady who was only capable of allowing me on her knee for a limited amount of time. After about ten years, Dad remarried and moved away to lead a well-deserved semi-comfortable existence after a miserable life of drudgery in the Wearmouth Colliery, which at that time was the world's deepest coalmine. He died in his early seventies from the miners' commonest complaint of silicosis. In this respect he fared well, because so many miners were carried away by it at a much earlier age.

On one occasion he showed me a terrible scar on his left leg running from knee almost to groin, resulting from a major rock fall at the coalface. It was almost two inches at the widest, where it had been crudely bound together, leaving him with a permanent rolling gait. This was one of the reasons for his move to Essex because he swore that none of his boys would ever work down the mine. He told us many stories of work at the coalface, including the fact that they had a long underground walk to reach the face and which must have taken them beneath the sea. He assumed this because they were constantly bathed in salt water that rained on them as they worked. The roofs of the coal seams at that time were supported by wooden pit props that needed constant renewal as they would split with a loud crack under the weight of the rock above them. Not surprisingly, therefore, there was a high rate of accidents from rock falls when the roofs collapsed.

Forestry, of course, was a thriving industry and Uncle Eddy was kept fully employed as a saw doctor just outside the pit gates. For some reason, which I never liked to ask, he lost an ear in an accident with a saw. The reader will be as puzzled as I am, as to how this could have occurred and no one within the family seemed to know or liked to ask him. In fact it was treated as a kind of secret joke. The common theory was that he was listening for a fault with a circular saw and forgot to switch it off.

Uncle Eddie was a sullen, morose Sheffield man of few words, in contrast to his wife Aunty Edie, who was Dad's sister and never stopped to draw breath. Eventually, during the war, they moved next door to us in a more modern house in Fulwell. His main love was concentrated on his cat and the budgie called Joey. Each evening after work he would sit with the cat on his lap after which it would sleep in the range oven when the fire died down. Joey's cage was permanently open and he spent most of the time running round Eddie's head and shoulders. Inevitably, the day arrived when one morning, he awoke to find Joey on his back in the bottom of his cage. For once Uncle Eddie showed some emotion as he held him in one hand and stroked his little breast with the other. As the tears flowed, he just kept repeating, "Poor Joey". He then carefully laid out a sheet of newspaper and neatly wrapped him in it. Finally he gently applied an elastic band to hold the makeshift shroud in place, before flushing him down the toilet or "netty".

Aunty Edie was a tiny, long-suffering woman, with a fiery temperament. In all fairness, her patience was sorely tested with Uncle Eddie. She often told him that one day she would run away and leave him. In reply, he would tell her that there was no need to run and she should take her time.

Dad's injury from the rock fall at the face also cost his friend Jim Peacock one of his legs with serious damage to the other. Jim lived next door and, surprisingly, was allowed to stay in his two-up-two-down terraced cottage by the generosity of the pit owners. He was even provided with a two-wheel trap and a pit pony called Molly who was due for early retirement, and this allowed him some mobility. In fact, Molly once provided an ambulance service with her cart for my eldest brother John, when she carried him to the hospital after he collapsed in the street with a burst appendix. John was as hard as nails and a lesser mortal would surely have died. His abnormal strength also served to fortify him in many hardships later in his

23

life. His nickname locally was "Oxo" Dixon in deference to his beefy strength and he once carried a heavy cooker for nearly a quarter of a mile on his back.

In contrast to John, who was short and stocky, my other brother Leo, who was always called Len, was tall and thinner. He was equally sturdy however, as a result of the harsh environment where only the fittest could survive.

I will not bore my readers with a lengthy description of a miner's cottage of the time, because many similar, but modernised ones are still in existence throughout the mining areas of the midlands and the north. Almost all of them have their foundations in the industrial revolution. In its earlier form conditions were much more primitive. The small concreted yard at the rear led to a dry toilet that backed onto the rear wall separating it from a narrow access lane shared by another row of cottages behind. A trapdoor in the "netty" wall at the back gave access into the "midden" to allow the waste to be shovelled out. The "scavenger" who did his round with a horse and cart in the middle of the night performed this thankless task. A simple verse we learned – almost from the cradle, ran:

> *The moon fell on the midden hatch,*
> *The scavenger had a fit,*
> *The wind blew out his lantern*
> *And he fell among the shit.*

When his round was finished, his other duty was to walk round the streets with a stick and tap on the upstairs windows to wake up the men for the early shift down the mine.

It was jokingly said that the best time to use the netty was just before dinner, when all the flies were in the kitchen!

I can still picture the wash-house, just outside the back door. It housed a coal-fired boiler for the family washing. After adding soap flakes to the wash tub, the clothes were put into the nearly boiling water and pounded with a "poss". This was a large wooden dolly with a cross handle at the top and the kids would have to take turns using it to pound the washing. After rinsing, the clothes would be wrung out with a mangle – an upright device with large wooden rollers driven by gears and an iron wheel with a handle attached. Again, this was job for the kids and the exposed cogs and rollers would never pass today's Health and Safety regulations. Another junior task was to cut up old papers into convenient sized sheets and thread them on a loop of string to hang on a nail for use in the netty.

A galvanised metal bath hung on the outside wall, to be brought into the living room on Friday evenings and filled with water from the boiler. Dad would have his bath in this in front of the fire with one of the kids to scrub his back. Dignity was a luxury not afforded to mining families. There were, of course, pithead showers but he said these only provided a lick and a promise.

When he had finished, the kids were the next to climb in and, last of all, guess who! A further factor was that only cheap carbolic soap could be afforded and we lived in a very hard water area. Each candidate for the bath therefore, generated a further batch of soap scum, so the benefit for me was questionable.

On the subject of cleaning, it has to be said that we, and most other families, were extremely fastidious and hardworking in this respect. The girls in particular were allocated their specific tasks, which included washing the outside steps and polishing them with red Cardinal polish. The hearth was also cleaned and coated with "Black Lead" twice weekly, and the back yard and front pavement were swilled down with water. There was also the annual ritual of the spring clean, when all activities were redoubled, and this even extended to inner cleanliness. For this purpose a bowl of "Salts of Lemon" was prepared and everyone would have a small glass with a piece of lemon every morning. The solution was made from Epsom salts, strongly laced with squeezed lemons and slices of lemon floating in it. On first tasting, the shock to the system would cause the buttocks to clench. Shortly afterwards the reverse would be the case, and the treatment would continue until "cleansing" was complete.

One excellent feature of the cottage was the coal-fired hearth. Apart from warming the living room it also had an oven at the side, with a deflector to control the heat and two trivets on which pans or the permanent kettle of water could sit and be swivelled near to the fire. There was also a very long-handled fork for spearing a slice of bread and holding it up to the fire. Nothing ever made golden brown toast as good as this, with such a distinctive crunchy flavour. I think these hearths are still a feature in many cottages today.

Friday night was also the night for making stotty bread. When mixed, the dough was left near the fire to rise in a large earthenware dish, covered with a damp cloth, then kneaded and divided into small rounds before being baked in the fired oven. The wonderful yeasty aroma of baking was a real highlight of the week. I think the origin of the name stems from the bouncy texture of the bread, because as kids we would play at "stotting" a ball against a wall. Another possibility could be that it describes the way it was thrown onto the oven tray. The traditional stotty bread is still widely available in the north today.

While on the subject of food, a traditional Geordie dish is Pan Hackelty, not to be confused with Pan Haggerty, which is a cheese dish. The former is baked in the oven in a shallow dish and would have lamb chops, black pudding, liver and sausages in a thick onion gravy and topped with sliced potato. More often, due to budget, it was only made with sausages.

As is always the case, people are strengthened by adversity, and Jim's wife, Mrs Peacock, was respected as the mainstay of our small community and even delivered me into this world. Although she had no formal training in midwifery, she acquired her skills through long years of experience. It could be argued that this is perhaps the best possible way and I will be eternally grateful for her expertise! She was truly one of the unsung saints of her time and always sought to help others despite bearing the heaviest burden herself.

27

All families in the north-east at this time were large, partly to compensate for the high infant mortality, but also I suppose, because sex was the only release in such a dreary existence. Beer, of course, provided another means of escape and was cheap in the miners' clubs. Geordies are still formidable drinkers and Vaux was Sunderland's own brewery, producing the most excellent "Double Maxim" ale.

My father always boasted that his brothers and sisters could form two football teams, if only they had all survived. Following local tradition, the boys were named after the Gospel Saints, starting – Matthew, Mark, Luke, John etc. The fourth one was Dad who was always known as Jack. When they ran out of saints, imagination would take over, particularly in the case of the girls. High infant mortality was a common outcome of this kind of lifestyle and less than half their children survived. Maybe just as well, because they also lived in a two-bedroom miner's cottage. As a result of the high birth-rate, it was always assured that there would be an ample supply of labour to feed the pits, because it is a fundamental law of nature that stress triggers an overwhelming instinct for procreation. And so it is the world over, when common sense decrees that the reverse should be the case. Mother Nature does, indeed, seem to have a cruel sense of humour from which we have no defence!

Our family, in contrast to most others, was relatively small, with three sisters followed by two brothers, and then me, following eight years behind the rest. There was a firstborn who was a boy and died in childbirth.

I think the reason for our small family lay in Mother's poor health caused by overwork. Finally, at a relatively young age, she suffered a stroke, which crippled her for a few years before she finally died when she was forty-five.

A couple of years after his accident, Dad wisely decided to move down south into Essex. As there were two boys between my sisters and me, I tended to consider them more maternally than sisterly, especially as I was only five when Mother died. My eldest sister Gladys was in fact eighteen years older than me and Edith, the youngest girl, fifteen years older. They were all married to Durham lads who had followed them to Essex.

As well as the eldest, Gladys was the largest, although by no means obese. She always dressed very smartly and was, perhaps, a little too heavy with her make up and use of cosmetic jewellery. Despite her somewhat tarty appearance, she had a heart as big as a whale and could always be relied on for help when needed. Her husband Jack was older by a few years and they were totally devoted to each other, and whisky, for which they seemed to have an infinite capacity while still remaining sober. Before moving South, Jack was a riveter in the shipyards followed by a career in the army.

The middle sister, Madge, had short dark hair and was attractive, even without the use of cosmetics. She had quite a shy nature and was generally reluctant to make social contact with strangers. When the ice was broken however, she was very friendly with a keen sense of humour. Although quite "careful" with money, she was extremely generous to her friends and family.

Edith was the youngest and also the smallest of the three girls and had probably the most serious temperament. She was of slim build with black hair and again, showed generosity to the rest of the family. She had a tendency to indecisiveness however, and frequently looked to the others, and particularly her younger brother Len, who was her favourite, for guidance. Her husband Jack started his working life in Sunderland as a butcher in a business where the stock was slaughtered in the yard at the back of the shop.

Typical of the family girls, they were all bosom buddies when together and quick to criticise each other when apart. Together however, they formed an alliance from which no one was safe.

As mentioned earlier, John was short and stocky and a likeable rogue who seemed to attract trouble. Much of this was due to his liking for drink, which he couldn't hold and got him into several fights. He was a hard case however and would not be beaten, as he seemed impervious to pain and would always go back to 'finish it'. In addition, he was a hard manual worker and a keen rugby player. He was well suited to his final occupation as a pub owner, where he had to deal with the occasional difficult customer and was into many shady deals. His hard way of life landed him in hospital on numerous occasions for a variety of operations, including three hernias and a perforated stomach ulcer.

Len, on the other hand, was just as hard, but

channelled his talents into more law-abiding pursuits like football and boxing. He even joined the police force, a career that almost terminated before it started, because with John, he was involved in a fight with some locals to which the police were called. This was on the very night before he was due to report for duty. He was in the police force for about two years before deciding that it wasn't for him.

I remember my pre-war days in Romford with great fondness. At that time, it was a bustling little market town with a cattle market and as the train approached from London, the first glimpse you had was the lovely towering spire of St. Edward's church.

Sadly, today the cattle market has given way to an extension of the market stalls and the ugly modern developments have totally surrounded the church that is almost hidden away in a corner as if it were an embarrassment.

Even as a small child I was free to wander at will because they knew I would always return when I felt the pull of food. Romford was then a town of great character full of exciting places to be explored. A regular venue however, was the cattle market and I well remember one occasion when a bull broke loose causing pandemonium, before it was finally captured in Woolworths.

At the top of the market stood the Laurie Cinema, a large square building that was the local flea-pit. Its big attraction was that it was cheap, offset by the fact that comfort had to be sacrificed. Almost all of the seats had a single large spring protruding through the torn upholstery, but with a little practice you could centralise it on your bum and wiggle the hips to work it down. It did, however leave a circular mark on the skin for some time afterwards. On the rare occasions when you had to queue, the line went down the side next to three thin fire doors, so that you could hear the sound track before you went in.

I went to the kids club every Saturday morning to see cowboy films starring Tom Mix and Gene Autry in between film breaks. As the projector was being rethreaded, the hoots and jeers were silenced by a burly youth who walked down the aisle clouting any trouble-makers. This, of course, only encouraged the ones behind him, so that the film breaks were the most entertaining part of the show.

Almost opposite Ind Coope's Brewery in the London Road was the Golden Lion, which was Romford's oldest pub and originally a coaching inn. The yard at the back once housed the stables, one of which was converted to a urinal and renowned for being one of the most foul smelling in the county and only capable of being used by the most inebriated. The Auction Rooms were in North Street just at the end of the yard and if you walked quickly, you could just hold your breath long enough to use it as a short cut.

The war, however, brought a series of changes from which the town was destined never to recover. Strange therefore, that I should now find myself back in the north, living with my married sister, her husband and baby son, in a place where life was in every way just as dangerous as the London blitz at its worst.

I think the reasoning for my transfer lay in the fact that the family was now being fragmented, with most of the men folk being conscripted in the forces. John, in particular, was in the Air Force as a heavy lorry driver and was soon posted to North Africa in the desert. True to his nature however, he was involved in some trouble with the local population and spent some time in the military prison. He seemed to enjoy this as it proved to be quite a soft option and only amounted to being confined to barracks. He was posted back home soon after.

Someone probably had the mistaken belief that it would be safer for me up north, but it probably had more to do with convenience, as I was so much younger than the others. I bear no resentment for this however, because I drew some comfort from living in Sunderland, which housed so many of my relatives.

There was a problem however, which I took with me to the north and this was a partial deafness accompanied by severe earaches. I suffered with this from a very early age and bouts would last for several hours with onset of frequent periods of dull aching and a rushing and pounding sound which built up to a sharp stabbing pain. Eventually relief would come when I fell asleep from exhaustion. When at primary school, I had to sit at the front of the class next to the teacher, who would bend down and speak very clearly to me and make sure I understood. I can't now remember her name, but I thank her sincerely for her patience at such a critical time in my education.

Shortly after arriving in Sunderland, I was seen by a specialist, who diagnosed that the problem was caused by abnormally large tonsils which should be removed with the adenoids. I vividly recall this operation as ether was used for the anaesthetic. I was held down by two nurses, one holding a stout cloth over my chest and arms, and another over my legs. I remember a cold pad being placed over my face and the peculiar smell, which only allowed me to breath out. Finally I went out fighting suffocation without being able to move. Perhaps the worst part of the operation however, was waking up and retching, with my throat on fire. Apparently this is a well-known side effect of the use of ether. Bouts of this retching continued into the second day with the throat bleeding every time. Ether is not now used as an anaesthetic for this reason. John had his appendectomy and first of three hernia operations with ether and the pain of violent retching with sutures in the abdomen must have been agonising. I think this probably hardened him to pain for the rest of his life.

4

Melancholy Thistle

Cirsium heterophyllum

Living alone with my elderly father in Essex seemed a strange affair and was almost a hand to mouth existence. Looking after each other meant that we had a very close relationship however, and it was at this stage of my life that I benefited most from his considerable experience.

The war continued to make life hazardous, but in a different way. Air raids were now largely replaced with firstly, the V1 "doodle-bug", and later the V2 rockets which could strike anytime during day or night. Although the V2s were more destructive, I found them slightly less frightening because they arrived without warning and when you heard the explosion you knew you had escaped. There was still the nagging doubt however, that the next one could have your name on it without you knowing. The V1 on the other hand, had a frightening monotonous droning sound and their ugly black shape, with short stubby wings and flames belching out behind, could easily be seen as they came mostly in daylight. Worse still, the engine would suddenly stop and you could see it coming at you. Despite all this we seemed to get by, with me taking the daily eight-mile bus journey to school and Dad working in a local factory in the boiler room. Food was still a problem, but now Dad could eat at work and school dinners were available at the government-run British Restaurants. It has to be said however, that eating in them was quite a risky affair, because the name of the dishes often defied their description. On one occasion I suffered a bad attack of food poisoning from a fairly nice-tasting paste, which was optimistically called "Shepherd's Pie". This was a regular feature on the menu, presumably because it was a convenient dish for using up leftover scraps after heavily masking the flavour with large amounts of onion. Fortunately both Dad and I were fairly adept at cooking whatever we could get hold of and we were also able to grow quite a lot of our own food.

Under his tuition I first learned how to keep rabbits, which provided an excellent free source of meat. He taught me the different qualities of each breed including the ones which gave the best meat and how best to kill and prepare them. Favourite breeds were the Flemish Giant and English Large White, because as the name suggests, they quickly put on weight and could provide enough meat to easily feed a family. It seems surprising that there doesn't seem to be a market today for tame table rabbits, although the smaller Chinese ones are available frozen. In terms of flavour these don't stand comparison.

Rabbit keeping proved to be quite profitable for me in later years when my sister Edith and her husband

Jack had a butcher's shop that provided a ready market for them. It became quite a routine after school to walk around the neighbourhood with a sack, collecting almost any kind of greenery suitable for their fodder. This was supplemented with a cheap readily available bran meal to provide roughage and give them a balanced diet. Dad also had a ferret, and used it to catch wild rabbits as a service to local farmers. He taught me how to clear a warren and peg down the purse nets over the exits before putting in the ferret, which startled them to run out. We would then remove them from the nets and give them a quick despatch. A good warren could yield about fifteen rabbits and of course, there was a ready market for them.

Our large garden also gave me my first interest in growing vegetables and the government's "Dig for Victory" campaign provided excellent literature and support to stimulate the imagination. For fertiliser, diluted urine was an excellent free source of nitrogen for those crops, particularly greens and leeks, which demand it – applied to the soil of course! It was also used as an activator to speed up the decomposition process in a compost heap, which would be used to improve the soil.

I think Dad was proud and pleased that I was getting an education, which was denied him through his restricted circumstances and lack of opportunity. He was totally devoid of sophistication and never lost his broad Geordie accent, even after living in Essex for several years. His accent was so broad, that my future wife Joan could hardly understand him, and I would often act as interpreter! Little did he realise however, how much wisdom he passed on to me. There were two maxims, which he would often quote to me and I can picture him saying them now. They were: "The man who never made a mistake never made anything," and "What one fool can do, so can another". In my later career years these have inspired me to attempt many things that I felt were far beyond my capability, merely because I knew some other "fool" could do it. As is often the case, wisdom has its roots in naivety and I remain in awe of him.

As with most Geordie men (and often women) he was quite a regular drinker, although I cannot ever recall seeing him even tipsy. He often took me to the pub with him and gave me my first beer at the tender age of five. His philosophy was that, "If they like it when they're young, they won't when they're older." Occasionally he talked a load of crap!

Although I knew he was proud of me, he never openly praised me for my achievements, but we had a kind of mutual understanding, and I just knew when I pleased him, and this was enough to encourage me to strive further.

In common with most northern miners, he was keenly interested in whippets and bred them for racing. On many Sundays in the north he would take his dog to meetings up on the fells where most of his friends congregated. The races themselves were very serious affairs involving complicated handicapping and classi-fication rules. In later years he patiently tried to explain them to me but frankly, they went far above my head. Despite all this the atmosphere was friendly and quite a lot of betting was involved, albeit quite illegal at the time. Such was their passion for the sport that it took place in all weathers and exposure to the raw biting winds on the fells is an experience not to be forgotten.

After moving to Essex, where there wasn't the same interest in this breed of dog, he switched to fox terriers and became quite an expert on their pedigrees. He tried to pass this on to me, but I never seemed to share his enthusiasm. As a lucrative sideline he would also use them on farms for rat catching, which is a natural instinct for a terrier. His love of dogs was the link that finally attracted him to his second wife who was a Crufts judge. Their common interests resulted in a comfortable marriage, based on genuine companionship but in his later years, he increasingly showed a tendency to want to be with his family. It almost seemed that he knew he had only a short time left.

Sadly, I was not to be with him when he breathed his last, because it happened suddenly and without warning. He had suffered from severe breathing problems for quite a few months and had paid a couple of visits to family members back in Sunderland after an absence of several years. When he returned from these, his breathing was much improved due to the fresher air and bracing climate. This then, is my epitaph to Dad, which again has its source in *Gray's Elegy* and so succinctly describes a life of poverty and hardship stoically borne.

Fair Science frowned not on his humble birth
And Melancholy marked him for her own.

I've since wondered if perhaps he was feeling an instinctive pull back to his roots in Sunderland in those last few weeks. I find a great empathy with him each time I return to the North, especially when, after leaving Washington Services on the Great North Road and rounding a bend, I am greeted by that magnificent statue of the Angel of the North. It so beautifully sums up that strength and dignity of the northern people who have suffered so much in the past. At the same time it conveys a sense of peace tinged with great pride.

I first decided that I wanted to pursue a career as a chemist when at the age of eleven I had a chemistry set as a Christmas present. Reading the booklet and following the reactions in the test tubes and crucibles I was transfixed and filled with wonder and when I went to live with Dad, a golden opportunity presented itself. Upstairs we had a small box room that could have been a third bedroom but was then unused. A crudely constructed bench and shelves formed the basis of my laboratory with a spirit lamp serving as a Bunsen burner.

At that time chemicals and equipment were fairly easily obtained and I was able to bury myself in catalogues from Gallenkamp in East London who still provide a large range of scientific glassware. Hopkin and Williams, of Chadwell Heath, also provided a wide range of laboratory chemicals. Additionally, the local library had a great range of basic chemistry books aimed at stimulating a young mind.

At this point it should be mentioned that, although I had a genuine thirst for knowledge of the natural sciences, not all my practices were innocent or even possibly legal. One particular fascination I had was with explosives and in particular those used as detonators. One of these could be painted on surfaces such as door handles and although quite harmless, would give a loud bang when touched. On one occasion, fortune must have smiled on me when I was unsuccessful in nitrating a small quantity of glycerine. If it had gone as planned it could easily have blown my hand off and caused major damage to the house. Another favourite preoccupation was the fermentation of various fruits to give wines that could then be distilled to yield quite potent spirits. One of my attempts with this was with elderberries. After crushing the berries they yielded a beautiful rich red coloured juice that I fermented with baker's yeast. A violent bout of sickness and diarrhoea however, quickly killed all my enthusiasm for this branch of science.

5

Flowering Cherry

Prunus spp.

The first two years in my new school were happy enough, considering the fact that our country was still at war and I was living alone with Dad. Although the standard of education in the south was higher than that in the north and particularly at the grammar school level, I seemed to take to it very well, remaining within the top few in the class, at least in those subjects that mattered. As mentioned earlier, it was now that I first became interested in science and had decided that I would like to pursue a career in chemistry.

It was a mixed school and of course, there was quite a lot of pairing and break-ups of the boys and girls. Strangely enough, there never seemed to be any pairing of boys and girls within the same class. I suppose it's like a marriage and there isn't the same excitement when you see someone every day and it's nice and comfortable to be just friends. In fact boys would often discuss their emotional problems with the girls in the class in an almost brother-sister relationship.

The later years were much easier with the ending of the war, although food was still rationed and most things were in short supply. Added to the necessary domestic chores was now the ever-increasing volume of homework as the exams approached but I seemed to cope well enough.

Some of the highlights of the year were the school dances. This of course was the era of the formal ballroom dance and most of us were quite good dancers. They were much more exciting for both sexes and gave the opportunity for close contact, often with a fair amount of fumbling and groping when out of sight of the ever-vigilant teachers. The playing fields and dark corridors of the school were ideal "snogging" locations, as also were the stairwells, (a bit over-populated and with limited space) and the sports department, which was eventually locked up. As far as I am aware however, there were never any teenage pregnancies. Such a difference today.

The boys in the class were friendly enough, but as always there were a few who were closer than the others and the inevitable cliques would form. Our small group always seemed to be at the forefront when there was any trouble, although we were academically bright. Corporal punishment was still practiced, but it was now administered by belt across the backside in the privacy of the headmaster's office and in the presence of the deputy head. It posed little problem for hardened criminals like us, especially when a little extra padding could be added inside the trousers. Again, we never felt any sense of unfairness and respected our headmaster. I think this was also reciprocated, and everything was conducted in quite an amicable atmosphere.

Hormone development was by now a raging force. On many occasions a boy would come into morning class and loudly proclaim that he could "produce the necessary". This would be a great point of discussion, and cause us all to compare notes, with some giving knowing looks and acting worldly wise, while others wondered what they were missing and if anything could be wrong with them. As far as I know, the girls never had such frank discussions, but I'm probably being naive.

It was during this next phase of my life that I first 'lost it', and in the most unexpected and delightful of circumstances. I'd already had an assortment of girl-friends from school, but nothing ever progressed beyond some mild petting. On a school trip to Switzerland in a village on Lake Lucerne however, it all happened.

At fifteen, after managing to master the elements of the grammar, I had reached a fairly reasonable standard in German. Unlike the rest of my classmates, I had no reticence in practising my limited conversational ability in Switzerland and I was therefore warmly received and greatly encouraged by the local people, particularly the girls.

Marguerite was about two years older than me and served in the local café on the large ferry landing stage by the lakeside. The venue was frequented by most of the local young folk and all our party was made welcome and we would meet there most evenings.

She was a stunning brunette with her hair curling

naturally over her shoulders, framing a full smiling face and soft brown eyes. Her appearance was not dissimilar to Ingrid Bergman, who was the current film beauty at the time and, together with Gina Lollobrigida, helped many a young boy through puberty! As if this were not enough, Marguerite had the most fantastic figure with full breasts, which strained to almost bursting out of her short black working dress. Over this she wore a small white apron. I think she was attracted by my attempts to converse in her language, and for my part I think the attraction was obvious! Under these circumstances an intense infatuation developed, and we would meet separately from our group after her work was finished in the evenings. We needed only to walk a short distance from the village to reach a dark deserted spot by the lakeside. The nights were warm, and the twinkling lights of the villages across the lake and the solitary chalets up in the mountains, when reflected in the water, made a magical, enchanted backdrop. The dream-like atmosphere was also enhanced by the occasional faint tinkling of a distant solitary cowbell.

Needless to say, our affair intensified and quickly developed to various forms of intimacy as we lay on our spread-out coats on the grassy bank beside the lake. As well as being two years older then me, she appeared to be the more experienced and I was unquestionably eager to learn. After some 'accidents' due to my over-excitement, her patience and encouragement finally rewarded me with the most unforgettable sensation of my life. She also seemed to have little concern about contraception and reassured me, so I assumed in my innocence that she had attended to those details. Very probably however, by the time the deed was consummated, I was "firing blanks". Those precious few nights with Marguerite will always remain in my thoughts.

My standing with the rest of the lads now increased further, although I can honestly say that I never boasted or divulged any details. Apart from the fact that I was late returning to the hotel, I can only assume it was the smug expression, or the halting gait caused by a lingering soreness. My German teacher once told me that the language would come in very useful some day. Little did he know!

Inevitably the two-week trip came to an end and it was with great sadness that we tearfully had to part. As I left she gave me her photo, which gave me a constant reminder of our affair. The train journey home was heart wrenching, as every mile tore me further away from her. At the same time I had to adopt an air of normality with my classmates. It was not to be the end however, as we promised to write regularly and I resolved to return as soon as circumstances would allow.

Unfortunately this never came to fruition, but our correspondence continued for the next two years or so with my German constantly improving. I eagerly anticipated every letter from her, in its pale blue envelope lined with dark blue tissue and written on fine quality pale blue paper. A romantic affair provides a wonderful focus when trying to master a foreign language.

Inevitably our letters became less frequent and I

finally lost her address, as well as her photo that I had treasured so much. I have no idea how I came to lose it when it was so dear to me, but I still carry a vivid image of it in my mind. It was a sepia print on an expensive cream coloured paper, with a deckled edge and slightly smaller than a postcard. The photo itself showed her head and shoulders with a hint of a smile and was of a professional standard with a fine textured silk surface.

I returned to the same lakeside village a few years later but found no sign of Marguerite and the magic of the location had disappeared. The local folk were also unable to help with my enquiries and although I enjoyed my second visit, the memories left me with a sad empty feeling. That hallowed grassy spot by the lakeside was still there, which redoubled the ache I was feeling.

Soon after that first visit we had the final leaving exam, which was the equivalent of today's GCSE. The main difference then was that, in order to pass, it was necessary to pass at least five subjects or the whole group had to be retaken.

Dad had promised me that if I passed, he would buy me my first bike and I'm pleased to say that I did rather well, with distinctions in seven subjects. I did however, fail in History. I never could summon up any interest in the terms of the Congress of Vienna, or how Europe was split up in the mid-nineteenth century, so my failure came as no surprise.

My prize was bought for ten shillings and needed a lot of work to renovate it. This was no disappointment for me and I spent many happy hours with my new interest. Virtually everything was lovingly replaced, repainted and chrome plated and I was justifiably proud of my efforts. What a wise choice he had made!

An additional stimulus was that, with three other classmates, we had planned a trip to Land's End via the north coast of Devon and Cornwall and returning along the south coast. This was meticulously organised weeks in advance, with stops every night in Youth Hostels. These were cheap but comfortable, with rough beds in large dormitories and rustic meals in generous proportions. They were exactly what were needed when we arrived exhausted and extremely hungry after a hard day's cycling. It was a great trip with lovely memories, although we lost a lot of weight from our daily exertions.

Another fond memory of this time was when I was fourteen and we went camping for a weekend. It all started when Freddie Firth said his brother Alan was on holiday, so we could use his tent, which would sleep four of us. I could also borrow his bike as I was the only one who didn't have one at that time. I just assumed he had his consent, so no questions were asked and I don't know if he ever found out. We had seen an ideal spot in a field leading to a quietly flowing river about five metres wide. The farmer was contacted earlier and we duly obtained his permission, even declining our offer of payment. He also obligingly dug a hole for us to use as a latrine.

So on the Friday evening we set out fully loaded up for the ten-mile journey in fine dry weather. Although complete novices, we made a reasonably easy job of putting up the tent and the evening meal of corned beef, boiled potatoes and baked beans wasn't too bad either. The village with its shop was only about fifteen minutes walk across the field and along a quiet lane. We found this useful for any odd items of food we had forgotten to bring with us. As a small group, we formed a team with a good spirit of companionship, so that all chores were shared equally without any kind of preplanned rota. We drew all our water for washing and cooking from the river, assuming, perhaps rashly, it was clean enough to drink.

One highlight of the weekend was the bathing afforded by the river and I have wonderful memories of four of us stark naked in the warm water at midnight by the light of a full moon.

On the Sunday afternoon, Paul Taylor's current girlfriend arrived with her friends and we were having a great time, except that Paul and partner got into some quite heavy petting and disappeared for some time. Apart from his handsome features and black curly hair that gave him a kind of Mediterranean look, Paul was a talented pianist and was considered quite a pull with the girls. One thing we found a bit irksome however, was the fact that he would boast of his exploits in graphic detail to us, although we suspected that much of it was exaggerated. We used to say to him that he had a "Mouth like Moby Dick and a dick like Mickey Mouse", but this was probably out of jealousy and it didn't deter him.

Eventually it was getting late and the girl's irate father arrived to take her home. In any case, this signalled the time for us to strike camp, and we finally got back home late on Sunday night to be ready for school the next day. We all agreed that it was a great weekend and we would do it again, but Freddie's brother Alan returned home and there never seemed to be another opportunity.

Inevitably and sadly, with all the final exam results in, the time came to leave school. Most of us, including myself, would take up jobs involving further training and a few would go to university. Traditionally the last day ended with a leaving ball that was quite a formal affair, with everyone making a special effort to look smart in his or her best clothes. Paul in particular, as an accomplished pianist, was to perform a couple of the numbers with the band and in deference to the occasion, turned up in his father's formal dress suit complete with tails. For some reason, the logic of which escapes me, there were pockets in the tails, which on such an occasion could only invite malicious attention.

As the evening drew to a close, the lights were dimmed and the last waltz was played as many new romantic affairs were started. Paul's relationship with his girlfriend had now developed to a serious stage and as they danced closely together, they were quite transfixed with each other. It was at this point that their tender moment was shattered as the jumping cracker exploded in one of the pockets in his coat tails, blowing it apart and ruining his father's suit. Needless to say, no one saw anything and the culprit was never found. I had the distinct impression in fact, that some of the staff shared the humour of the situation, although of course, an inquiry was undertaken for the sake of his father.

6

Baby Blue Eyes
Nemophila menziesii

Although somewhat crowded, our rented terrace house in Essex was almost luxurious compared with the miner's cottage. To begin with there was a bathroom and separate toilet upstairs and a tiny third bedroom. Somehow two sisters and husbands, two brothers, Dad and of course me, managed to get by, although it was pretty much a case of each one fending for themselves.

As the youngest of six by eight years, I was very much the baby of the family and often came in for quite a lot of flak from my older brothers and sisters. After school I was used as a convenient shopping service, constantly running errands to the shops, often for cigarettes and quite trivial items. This was not so bad except that it was a non-stop chore, because I usually had to return for odd forgotten items. Since I was at the beck and call of my sisters as well as brothers, my services were constantly in demand. In particular, as there was no fridge, everything had to be bought in small quantities and with so many living in the house, I often had to fetch the same items before school in the morning and then in the afternoon.

My brothers Len and John often doled out punishments, which I thought were unfair, although I later realised they were probably teaching me to look after myself. One secondary effect of this however, was that it made me resentful and often quite devious. At one time some boys were throwing stones at a small group of my friends and I was hit on the forehead by a large piece of brick. I returned home with blood pouring down my face and Len was told to go and find out who did it. Since it put him to some inconvenience however, he gave me a resounding wallop before he left "for letting them do it".

As I was no physical match for my brothers, I eventually developed more subtle ways of defence, and on this occasion an opportunity for revenge presented itself a few days later. I had a few "caps" for use with a toy gun. These were small discs about 5mm in diameter with an explosive charge sandwiched between layers of paper. When placed in the gun, they gave out a loud bang when struck by the trigger hammer.

Len had gone out somewhere and left his opened packet of cigarettes on the table. I removed only three of them and managed, with a great deal of patience and a pin, to slide a cap between the tobacco and the paper in each one. I then replaced them in the packet in random order. The following Sunday evening as usual he went to the cinema on his own, and while watching the film he lit one of his cigarettes. After three or four minutes there was a resounding bang, which blew the cigarette to pieces and sent sparks

The Family in the Early Fifties

Dad

Gladys   Madge   Edith

John   Len   Me

The Monkwearmouth colliery where Dad worked. Now the site of the Stadium of Light.

Landing the herrings. A risky occupation in wartime yet sold cheaply.

Seaburn beach finally cleared of mines. Our football pitch was on the right.

Barrage balloon in the docks for defence against dive bombers.

The photos above were reproduced by kind permission of *The Sunderland Echo*.

This was The Blue Bell hotel – just over 200 yards from our house.

Bomb damage in the docks.

Both of these houses were in Sea Road near our school and ten minutes walk from home.

The Queen Alexandra Bridge with the shipyards underneath on the right. The disused rail track over the road housed anti-aircraft guns and searchlights – a prime target.

Student Days.

Biker Boy.

Early married life.

Joan in that first car.

flying from the glowing end. The audience found it hilarious and he was acutely embarrassed and too scared to light up another one. Surprisingly, he let me off quite lightly, so I think he must have appreciated the subtlety and ingenuity of the plot.

It's a well-known scientific principle that if there are two forces stronger than you, the best defence is to use them against each other. This was made easier for me by the fact that both Len and John had fairly short tempers. One such opportunity I have in mind was presented because they shared the same bedroom and their socks and underwear were in separate piles in the same cupboard. This caused frequent quarrels; because if one hadn't done his washing, he would help himself from the other pile causing the complaint that he was a lazy bugger, leaving the other to do all his washing. The rows were finally settled with the agreement that John would put a stitch of red wool in all his items. Anything without stitches would therefore belong to Len. The arrangement eventually broke down when John bought new pants and hadn't got round to putting the stitch in, so Len took them for his own. The ensuing battle was now settled with the agreement that Len would now mark all his socks and underwear with green wool. This was the very opportunity I had been waiting for. When they were both at work, I cut the red stitches from some of John's pants, replaced them with green, and placed them in the other pile. The resulting row was quite a bitter one that I found most satisfying, with each one accusing the other of dishonesty. It gave me a warm glow and delightful sense of justice. Of course I pleaded innocence and said

I knew nothing about their arrangement. I don't think they ever resolved the cause of the problem.

On another occasion, John was sucking petrol from his work's lorry to siphon it off with a hosepipe into a can. Quietly creeping up behind him, I slapped him hard on the back, causing him to swallow a mouthful. Needless to say, I was a very fast runner and we both knew he couldn't catch me. Thankfully, he had mellowed when I came home some hours later and although he had been burping petrol all day long, I got off with a caution.

A very unpleasant condition, which beset my early teenage years, occurred over a period of several weeks. It started with a small sore spot on the back of my neck where the shirt collar rubs. It took a few days to form a head, during which time it became extremely painful before finally bursting. By this time however, another had started to form followed by a succession of much larger ones. These boils were extremely tender even on light contact and still worse; they had spread to the small of my back where the belt rubs.

Modern antibiotics now ensure that onset of boils can easily be controlled by a short course of pills. As they were not then available, the treatments were rather more primitive and painful.

The first of these was applied after a head had formed and before the boil had burst. It consisted of a medicated paste of china clay or kaolin supplied in a tin, which was immersed in a pan of hot water. When the contents were thoroughly heated, the paste or poultice, was spread onto a piece of cotton lint and applied to the boil, then tied with a bandage. The special property of kaolin is that it retains its heat for a long time. Bearing in mind that boils are very sensitive to the touch, the application of a very hot poultice is an experience never to be forgotten.

The next stage of treatment took place after the boil had burst and was used to draw out the infection, which had usually spread some distance from the centre. In this case a glass bottle was heated in the oven and the neck was then applied to the boil. As cooling occurred, a strong suction started, which drew the boil and its surrounding area inside and partly removed the infected material. This was repeated at regular intervals as needed – usually twice a day. I still bear the scars of this treatment on my back.

On one particular occasion, I was quite ill with a large "blind" boil on the back of my neck, which had simply grown larger and more painful over a period of a few days without coming to a head. As I was eating lunch my sister Madge said, "If it doesn't burst by this evening we'll go to the doctor and have it lanced". I remember that the food I had in my mouth set like a rock as all the saliva drained out. The thought of anyone touching it, let alone cutting it with a knife, is the stuff nightmares are made of. Fortunately, either by shock to the system or natural progression, the blessed relief came late in the afternoon. The misery of this disorder extended over a period of some months, as a fresh crop would start afresh after a brief respite from the previous ones. The irony of the situation was that antibiotics became available soon after the last ones had healed and boils are now either almost unknown or at most a minor inconvenience.

7

Poor Man's Orchid

Schizanthus pinnatus

Leaving school was an occasion of mixed emotions. On the one hand there was the sadness of leaving a comfortable, protected environment with the daily contact of close friends. Against this was the excitement and anticipation of beginning a life with new opportunities and challenges as well as new experiences whilst earning money as well.

With my good grades on leaving I had no trouble in securing a job as a trainee chemist in a chemical manufacturing works in East London. Although the pay was low, I was allowed a day off each week to attend college and the prospects seemed good. Additionally, however, the B.Sc. course required three evening classes per week and the associated homework demanded a total commitment stretching through the weekends.

After a year or so it became obvious that, although I still had a keen interest in the work, this regime had now become a treadmill which couldn't be sustained. A way out was finally found when, after passing the intermediate level exams, or Inter.B.Sc., I managed to obtain a small state grant to allow me to attend college and complete my studies. With my Saturday job doing van deliveries for the butcher's shop managed by my sister and her husband, I lived at just about subsistence level after paying a small token amount for my keep at home.

So now began an exciting new life as a full-time student, with my new friends who were also on the bread line. One of my closest friends in our group was an Irish lad called Pete McArthy or Mac. He had dashing good looks and with his soft Irish accent, he attracted the girls like a magnet. He would have "serious" affairs with girls for a few weeks by telling them blatant lies, and then ditch them in tears after cheating on them with the next temporary replacement. Surprisingly, most of the girls knew of his reputation and it in no way deterred them. He also confided in me that he was having an affair with a married lady who lived near the college, and I knew he wasn't boasting. All in all, Mac was a loveable rogue and we remained good friends for my entire time at college. On one occasion I recall, we were eating lunch and he had a ham salad. He suddenly stopped eating and pushed the food away because he remembered it was Friday. When I asked him what was wrong, he said his Catholic religion didn't allow him to eat meat on Fridays. I said to him: "As an utter reprobate, Mac, I'm surprised you can place any importance on rules laid down by your church". His reply was: "I'm know I'm a sinner Ron, and one day I'll be answerable. Also, I've very little respect for my church leaders and less still for the people in the congregation, but I feel I need to go every week and pay my respects to my Maker". A thought for us all maybe.

At about this time a memorable holiday was planned with three of my former workmates. As I had recently passed my driving test and as the only driver, we decided that we would all club together and hire a small car (a Ford Prefect) and do a fourteen day tour of Scotland. Funds of course were very tight, especially after allowing for fuel costs, so the plan was to sleep in the car and look for cheap B&Bs on alternate nights. Understandably, the worst place of all to sleep in a car is the driver's seat, where the limited space makes it impossible to get comfortable and the fairest solution was that we would take turns here.

The standard of some of the accommodation on the other nights reflected the price, but seemed luxurious compared with the car. To have running water and a prepared breakfast, however basic, was a real treat and the condition of the bedding doesn't seem to matter if you're tired enough.

The arrangements for ablution after a night in the car, were to drive out and find a mountain stream for washing and cleaning the teeth. Hot water for shaving was taken from the car radiator after which it was refilled from the stream. The scenery of course, though beautiful, was offset by the thousands of ever-present midges that bit us everywhere and raised large bumps that itched constantly. Surprisingly, after the first week, we never noticed them. Perhaps our systems had become immune to their bites.

On one memorable occasion, we arrived in Portree on the Isle of Skye at the same time as the Highland Games. It was our time to sleep in the car, which was just as well because there were no vacancies to be had. The only place suitable to park the car was in the town square outside the Police Station and we duly went inside to ask if it would be OK. After explaining our financial situation, the duty sergeant was very sympathetic to the fact that we "couldn't" find a place and agreed it would be the only solution. The most delightful thing of all however was that, at about nine o'clock, one of them came out with mugs of hot tea and suggested that two of us could use their cell for the night, which would be far more comfortable than the car. As it was my turn for the driver's seat, I was the first lucky one and the other was agreed quite amicably between them. Better still, after a lovely night's sleep on warm comfortable bunks, they sent us all on our way with large chunky bacon sandwiches and hot tea. I still owe them a debt of gratitude and I wonder if there are any police like that today.

Most of the science classes consisted of boys, and there were, in fact, only two girls who were totally dedicated to their studies and in any case were singularly unattractive, both physically and socially. If it were not for the girls from the Art department and keeping contact with work colleagues, courses in the scientific subjects would have been somewhat monastic. There were, however, two girls from my previous firm who now seemed to surface even though they were mere acquaintances before.

Joyce was a stunning petite blond with a slim figure

and a slight shyness that added to her attractiveness. Following the death of her mother at an early age, she lived with her grandparents about fifteen miles from where I lived in Romford. The situation regarding her father was a delicate matter and she seemed reluctant to talk about it, so I avoided the subject. Our affair lasted a few months and although we greatly enjoyed each other's company we both seemed to not want intimacy to go beyond some mild petting. In the end it seemed to die a natural death and we would see each other a little less often. I also began to find her shyness a little oppressive and we seemed to have exhausted all the common ground between us.

Olive worked in the sales office and was a brunette with a slightly more buxom figure than Joyce. Added to this, her main attraction for me was her soft brown eyes and full lips that promised such rousing, passionate kisses. From the start I was quite flattered by the intensity of her feelings that were in total contrast to Joyce. After some time however, I found her a little too intense, especially when she frequently tried to surprise me with a string of small unsolicited presents which gave the impression that she was unnecessarily trying to buy my affection. Despite this, our affair lasted quite a few months during which time I found myself trying to slow things down as I wasn't prepared to commit so fully as she was. In all relationships it is necessary to keep a good balance where emotions for each other are equal or almost so. If it were not for the fact that Olive was too pushing, things may well have gone further.

While at work I had managed to save enough money

to buy a second hand B.S.A. motorbike, which saved the bus fares to college and offset some of the other travel expenses.

As well as giving me quite a bit of attention from the opposite sex, the B.S.A. was the pride of my life, although it was a somewhat love-hate relationship. The frequent maintenance demanded quite a lot of my time as it was not an easy machine, but the joy of driving it made it the more worthwhile. With a companion riding pillion, and sharing the expenses, I spent many happy days camping and touring – mainly in Devon and Cornwall.

Compared with the dress of today's biker, the appropriate clothing at the time seems quite minimal. In my own case I had a pilot's sheepskin flying jacket and goggles, bought from a war department surplus clothing store. The final flourish was the elbow-length leather gauntlets. With the goggles pushed up on the forehead for effect, I thought I looked quite cool, and it gave me serious pulling power with the girls! The hard helmet was not then a legal requirement and rather foolishly, I never wore one and even survived a few spills unscathed.

In 1953, Canvey Island suffered the most devastating flood in its history. Worst of all, it happened in February in bitterly cold weather. As students we responded to the call for helpers, and since I had the motorbike, I went with Mac as my pillion rider.

We crossed the bridge onto the Island in mid-afternoon, frozen from the ride on one of those dull, sombre February days. The main road was still passable – but only just. On either side the farmlands were flooded, with enormous bloated dead cattle floating by the roadside. It was an unreal, almost nightmare scenario, with only the two of us on the road and the silence broken only by the throaty noise of the B.S.A. engine. The Community Hall was the main centre of activity and when we arrived we were designated as crew to the rowing boats, searching for survivors on the bungalow roofs. With only the lines of roofs to give an indication of the streets, it was almost like being at sea with our return only guided by the distant light of the Community Hall. It was quite dark before we left the Island since we could be of no further use and, chilled to the bone, we faced the long ride home.

Student life itself was no easy ride and the state grant was always conditional on a good exam result at the end of each term. A further pressure came from the fact that we were all deferred from military service under the same conditions. In spite of this, we seemed to enjoy life well enough and freely shared all our meagre possessions, finding many ways of making economies. One such example was that we would take our coffee by sniffing a pinch of powdered Nescafe, which used far less and gave a new meaning to the term 'instant'. The aftertaste lasted at least as long as a cup of coffee. For the smokers, which included Mac and myself at the time, we rolled thin cigarettes with tobacco mixed with a generous amount of herbal smoking mixture. This was obtained very cheaply in a large bag from a local herbalist shop and had doubtful curative properties. As an alternative it could be taken in a pipe, but it crackled and tasted like a bonfire. Although very good for posing – we thought it looked quite cool and mature at the time – I've yet to find out what the constituents were. Quite popular at the time was the practice of growing your own tobacco. I didn't do this myself, but tried some grown by one of our lecturers, and I think that even the herbal mixture was preferable. At least it came from the right plants although the nicotine content was very low.

Some slight financial relief during this phase came from the Saturday job driving a delivery van for our butcher's shop. The hours were long, starting at 6 a.m. and finishing at 5 p.m. with no break and sandwiches to be eaten on the job. My van was a very old temperamental Ford which often needed quite a bit of coaxing with a starting handle to get it running, particularly on a cold winter morning. The starter motor was to be avoided, in case it drained the battery and then the whole day's deliveries would be lost. At six o'clock on a winter morning, it was still dark and the cold could be biting and painful for the hands.

Despite the hours, however, I found it enjoyable, especially as it led to a very pleasant intimate relationship with two of my customers. They were both sisters and extremely attractive, although they were about ten years or so older than me. Laura was an outgoing, fun-loving girl with a fairly full figure and short dark hair, whereas her sister Elsie was older by a couple of years and totally different. She was slightly taller and slimmer, with fair hair worn in a pony tail and had a much quieter personality that I found equally attractive. Both of them shared the same rented house and seemed to live alone. They appeared to be quite happy to share me and, all in all, it was a very amicable arrangement with each one discreetly finding an excuse to leave me with the other. They even insisted on paying their butcher's bill! They were new customers and, from our very first meeting, they flirted quite openly, making no secret of their intentions. I, of course, responded equally eagerly, and the affair quickly developed within a couple of weeks. On my second Saturday delivery call, they invited me back for an evening meal after I finished work and I readily accepted. After a bath and change of clothes, I duly turned up in the evening – on the B.S.A. and in my posing gear of course! It was then I learned that they both worked in catering, and they therefore treated me to a beautifully cooked dinner. Afters were even better!

The following day, being the Sabbath, it really was a much-needed day of rest from my labours. This arrangement continued for a few weeks until finally they found it necessary to move away to be with their mother in Yorkshire. We sadly parted on very friendly terms, although in truth there was no great depth of feeling on either side.

Christmas was also a busy time in the shop, as the poultry was delivered rough-plucked and in order to maintain freshness, could only be prepared shortly before collection. We would work through until two or three in the morning, drawing and preparing turkeys, geese and chickens, with my sister Edith fortifying us with tea, laced with brandy.

On one occasion we had a particularly mild spell at Christmas and our chickens started to take on a slight greenish hue with a clammy feel to the skin. In desperation I took a bag of flour in the van and dusted the birds before delivery. This whitened them and gave them a nice silky feel. After Christmas to my great surprise and without exception, everyone complimented me and said how much they had enjoyed their Christmas dinner!

It was also a particularly profitable time on my round, as many people kept chickens. Food rationing still continued for several years after the end of the war and even after that there were some shortages. Chickens were therefore kept by many people, both for the eggs and to ensure a good Christmas dinner. After looking after them, however, they didn't have the heart to kill them, and I would provide this service for them when I called on my round. I would then leave them plucking the feathers out, and call back later at the end of my deliveries to draw and prepare them for the table. My charge for this was half-a-crown each, which was reasonable but amounted to a sizeable sum for me in my straightened circumstances, and for what was quite a heavy day's work. I must admit that I am still uneasy about killing anything, as I was with the rabbits, but I console myself with the thought that I do give them a quick death, which is seldom the case when they die naturally.

At home we used our fairly long garden to advantage by keeping a dozen or so chickens and a couple of geese. I must admit, I have never liked geese, except on the table, and these two birds must have sensed it. Every time I went down the garden they would make a concerted attack and I would retaliate with a stick I kept handy as a weapon. I think they enjoyed the challenge of this because it seemed to spur them on to renewed aggression. Eventually I had my revenge at Christmas when it was time to have them for dinner. As Edith's husband Jack held one of them head downwards in order to break the neck, my job was to give it a bear hug to contain the wings. After death, however, as a nervous reaction the wings continue to flap for a short time afterwards, but I let go too soon. This was when I learned how strong a goose wing can be as it nearly broke my jaw. The outcome was that I ate my Christmas dinner with a swollen and painful face, so I suppose they finally had some kind of revenge.

8

Thrift

Armeria maritima

As my studies came to a conclusion I was now obliged to present myself for National Service. In preparation for this, I had earlier been interviewed and, after several tests, was provisionally allocated a suitable placement. I had always expressed a keen desire to fly and so I was pleasantly surprised to find that I had been accepted for aircrew training as a pilot or navigator. This was quite unusual for a National Service recruit and so I was rather looking forward to it.

During my last year at school I had virtually confirmed my desire to embark on a career as a chemist, but in preference to this I would have chosen flying. A great opportunity presented itself at the time when the school announced that, if anyone was interested, they could take the entrance exam for Dartmouth Naval College. As it would give me the chance to train for the Fleet Air Arm, I was delighted to apply, and did rather well in the exam so that I was called for an interview in London with three senior naval recruitment officers.

The interview itself went extremely well, until I was asked what rank my father held in the navy. When I told them he'd never been in the navy, the atmosphere chilled somewhat and I was thanked for attending. The result of course, was a foregone conclusion. I was quite disappointed and not a little resentful, because Dad's job as a miner had been equally, if not more challenging and dangerous than one in the navy. Presumably the offspring of land-based parents are unsuitable for a career at sea. It also raises the question that, if it was a key issue, why wasn't it featured on the application form? I suppose this is what is meant by military intelligence, a prime example of an oxymoron.

Now, however, another opportunity had arisen to take up flying, albeit not as a career, but it was at this stage that fate intervened and declared other plans for me. It started quite suddenly with a dark curtain that wafted from side to side and descended over the vision in my right eye. This quickly deteriorated to the stage where I almost lost all of the sight in it. My doctor was so concerned it might be a retinal detachment that he arranged my immediate admission to hospital and I was to be there for the next two months. After various tests it was diagnosed as a condition called choroiditis, and was treated with injections both intravenously and in the eye itself. The condition improved, although only slowly, with outpatient treatment over the next two years.

Needless to say, any form of National Service was not now an option, and so I was free to begin my career as a research chemist. It was also at this time that I got married. Joan was our secretary in my first job a few years earlier, and we had been seeing each other in a group on a casual basis since then. Our group of friends was formed from fellow students and workmates over a period of years and even extended to each other's families. One of our common interests was a love of music and every Friday evening during the promenade season we would, as a routine, go to the Royal Albert Hall for the Beethoven concerts that were a regular feature at the time. For the cheapest entry price we could sit on the floor on newspaper in the upper gallery with our backs propped against the wall, whilst the music transported us to another world. Similarly the operas at Convent Garden offered cheap entertainment on steeply tiered seats up in the gods. These were in the form of narrow benches set into the walls, with comfort secondary to the performance.

To start our married life, we were lucky to find a one-bedroom upstairs flat to rent until we could save enough for the deposit on a house. Because we had very little starting capital, we knew we would have to live quite frugally for the first two or three years.

As it turned out, we had to give up the flat after only two years, as the property was put up for sale, and we were forced to go house hunting with less capital than we would have liked.

After a frustrating and very extensive search we finally found a bungalow in a very nice rural location about one and a half miles from the town centre of Wickford.

At that time Wickford was a small country town, affectionately known locally as Dodge City, but full of character and where everyone knew each other. Two of the shops in particular were treasure chests of rural goods, such as purse nets for catching rabbits and all manner of fascinating agricultural hand tools. Even vegetable seeds were sold from sacks in small metal cup measures – beans by the half pint – and next to the animal feeds, baker's yeast was sold by the ounce and cut from a block for home baking. Live chickens were also auctioned alongside second-hand furniture in the yard next to the market and across the road next to The Castle pub.

The main road out of town to our house is now a modern highway with full street lighting and congested with traffic. It was then a country lane, only paved in some places, with lighting along the whole stretch to our home provided by three sixty-watt bulbs mounted on the telegraph poles. On many occasions the last bus from town required a push start from all the passengers and one bus in particular had a hole in the floor through which the tyre could be seen. If the last bus had gone and you had to walk, it was fairly certain that somewhere along the road, a car would stop and it would be one of the locals who you knew.

The price of the bungalow was also within our reach, firstly because the structure of the building was in such a poor state of repair and secondly, problems with the River Crouch had caused bad flooding in the town and its surrounding area. Fortunately, the bungalow and its environs were on higher ground and managed to escape the flood.

At least it was habitable enough to enable us to move in, and so began a two-year DIY rebuilding project. Our bungalow had the advantage of electricity, but some of our neighbours only had gas or oil and were saving to have it connected. Although I was reasonably competent with the more common domestic repairs, this was very much a learning process for me. Added to this was the fact that, although we were both working, materials were expensive and could only be bought when we had saved enough for them. It also put pressure on me not to waste them due to bad workmanship. We were helped in this respect by the presence of a second-hand wood yard nearby. In the end I enjoyed acquiring new skills like plumbing and plastering and got a great deal of satisfaction from it in spite of the relentless hours of work on top of the day job.

One of the most urgent jobs was forced on us because our first winter was particularly severe and I had snow blowing under the roof tiles and settling in the loft space, even covering the electric wiring. This had me up in the middle of the night shovelling out buckets of snow in case it melted and came through the ceiling. Fortunately I later managed to find some used tiles of the same type, which were in good condition and going fairly cheap.

The harsh winter and rural location meant that we suffered from several power cuts and many times we came home from work and had to spend the entire evening by candlelight. Nowadays it's considered quite romantic to use candles both for dining and even for taking a bath surrounded by them. From my own experience it evokes memories that offend all the senses. In the dim flickering light, I see condensation running down curved corrugated iron. I also recall the feel of cold, damp clothes, on my skin and the scream of Stuka dive-bombers together with the vile smell of burning rancid tallow fat. Of course, modern candles have no smell, unless they are deliberately perfumed, but during a recent power cut when it was necessary to use them, I found the whole experience far from romantic.

Another unwelcome task arrived when the bedroom floor collapsed, again in the middle of the night. This was due to a leaking back boiler causing the boards and joists to rot. Again I was lucky to have the second-hand timber yard fairly near.

Following this job we could turn our attention to the kitchen, which had to be re-plastered before constructing the units from flat packs. Alongside this the plumbing was virtually renewed, since the kitchen would incorporate a new multipoint gas heater, which also served the bathroom.

As funds became more available, I designed and built an attached garage, which housed our wreck of a car, although it certainly didn't deserve such luxury. It was a Standard 8 and a beast of a machine, which frequently broke down at the most inopportune times. That particular model was also called The Flying Standard but I think the designers must have had a very vivid imagination. I would not even have considered it were it not offered to us at such a very cheap price from Joan's father and refusal would have seemed ungrateful. The fact that he always seemed to be working on it was a sign of things to come. On one occasion I drove Joan to the station to go to work before going to work myself. It was early on a winter morning and still dark, and as I switched the lights to parking at the station, the whole of the switch assembly fell apart with springs and small parts falling to the floor. Needless to say, it took forever to piece it all together again and I finally drove back home holding it all in position with one hand, whilst trying to multitask with the other one. The car finally met its end when I used it to tow a friend's car into a breaker's yard. The greatest indignity came when he got £10 for his, but I was only offered £5 for mine! Due to shortage of funds, a succession of second-hand cars followed, which at least gave me good knowledge and experience as a mechanic.

As the time went by, we now began to enjoy a more comfortable life in our refurbished home. With less expenditure on the building, and progress at work, money became less of an issue and more was available for saving and occasional holidays. We were also able to take a more active part in the local community with Joan organising events for the elderly, and as secretary of the local gardening club, I ran the twice-yearly shows and barn dances as well as purchasing bulk materials for the allotment holders.

While on the subject of holidays, although I looked forward to and enjoyed them, I found them a bit of a routine after a while. At three per year we found that quite often we were simply revisiting the same places. Generally cruises were more favoured as they offered more variety coupled with unaccustomed luxury.

I'm now of the opinion that a person's life must be fairly mundane when the highlight of the year is a holiday, where people are treated like cattle at airports and often suffer frequent and uncomfortably long delays. Added to this, any available food and drinks at airports are both inferior and expensive. The most popular destinations by definition are overcrowded, which also means that the hotels, at best, are simply people processors and totally devoid of any character. Why people should pay so much, simply to buy stress, is beyond my understanding.

So now after twelve years and with my career as a research chemist progressing, we felt that the time was ripe to think about starting a family in a new home. After a year or so of house hunting and by a happy coincidence on our final cruise, we found that Joan was pregnant. Again the timing worked in our favour, as we moved into our larger detached house in October and our daughter Nicky was born just before Christmas that year.

One of the attractions of our new home was the half-acre, well established garden, which was south facing and afforded total privacy. As a keen gardener, I enjoyed the large garden in our last bungalow, but this was now in a different league, with its superb fertile soil and well-drained hilltop location. Additionally, it was barely a ten-minute drive away from the old place, so we were still able to maintain contact with all our old friends.

As my work was concerned with high-speed processing of photographic film, I was offered the opportunity to help in the development of a new process which would produce videocassettes based on microfilm on a commercial scale. Since there wasn't a video recording alternative at the time it seemed that its future was assured. Inevitably of course, it's in the nature of research that changes must occur. At the same time as the microfilm process was being developed, other systems using magnetic tape emerged, which proved to be more commercial, as they offered the advantage of rerecording. Strangely enough, there was still a market for a microfilm process, but mainly for the medical profession in Japan. This meant that the entire plant was sold out and exported and, with a decent redundancy settlement, I immediately started a new job in a chemical plant.

9

Bats-in-the-Belfry

Campanula trachelium

So began another phase of my career as manager of a chemical manufacturing plant with a crew of the most odd and interesting characters you could wish to meet. As with most organisations, there was a service team of men who did the hardest work and formed the backbone of the unit. Although classed as "unskilled", the knowledge and experience of such staff sometimes outweighs that of some of the higher grades. For personal reasons however, they never seem to show any desire for progression.

John was one particularly likeable character who joined the team as a result of the closure of the London docks. As an east-ender he had that typical easy-going outlook on life, with a natural sense of humour that was sharpened by the fact that he was extremely well read and self-educated. He was also an avid gambler who took everyone's bets to the local bookies every day during his lunch break. Over the years his mathematical skills had been honed to a knife-edge and he was able to calculate returns from the most complicated accumulator bets in an instant. As I was a very occasional punter, he would often try to persuade me to have a flutter with his usual saying. "Yer got t' speculate to accumulate. Nuffink grows in yer 'and – 'cept yer cock". On another occasion he said, "Told the missus if this double comes up, I'll treat her to a night out with a lesbian".

Big Dave was an easy-going giant of a man with the strength of an ox and under the strict control of his tiny wife who bore him four sons. On one occasion, as I was about to leave work, I found my car had a puncture. Since I had no jack, he offered to help by lifting the car up for me while I changed the wheel. Without showing the least sign of strain, he chatted away until the job was finished and he could set the car down again. The most fascinating thing I found about him was that he was a skilled artist and would create wonderful lifelike pencil portraits of his mates while sitting at his tea break. He could easily have earned a living as a professional artist with his talent. Unlike John, however, he was not gifted with the sharpest of minds and on one particular occasion at a union meeting, he seconded a motion to ban overtime working, then voted against it!

As a contrast however, there were others in the team who were not quite so well endowed. Richard was one such character – a proper Dick – who seemed to live on his nerves and spoke with a slight staccato stutter in his voice. Although he was unaware of it, he was known as "Road Runner" by the rest of the crew, who would make the distinctive "mi-mi" noise when he approached. He had previously worked as a hairdresser and used to cut hair for everyone in the crew. On one occasion, he was cutting someone's hair near the end of his shift when he was told to go home on some emergency. He quickly put his tools away and left his client with half a haircut until the following day. One day, he was in my office when his wife phoned to say how sorry she was that Richard was quite poorly that morning and unable to come to work. As I handed the phone to him his stutter became much worse with acute embarrassment.

Fred was a short, stocky, almost ape-like man who walked with a slight stoop and had the most unattractive facial features with thick lips and expressionless staring eyes. He lived alone and would bring his best clothes to work every Friday so that he could change at the end of his shift. He would then make his weekly pilgrimage to London to seek the services of a prostitute, despite the fact that he had been repeatedly treated for STDs. He said one of his "special" ladies plied her trade in Wapping and would service her customers in an alleyway against a wall. Always a charmer, he told us that she charged five pounds and they would both hold the note between forefinger and thumb and he would only release it when satisfaction had been achieved! I am of the opinion that the ladies who trade in sex provide a useful, possibly essential service for men like Fred. If their profession was recognised and accepted, as in other countries, it would be the more easily controlled and there would be far fewer cases and risk of STDs. Poor Fred must have been driven by strong forces to accept those risks. It simply flies in the face of our narrow-minded prejudices that outlaw mankind's oldest profession. "Judge not, that ye may be judged". Live and let live.

Harry lived a solitary life in a country cottage and since he spent most of his life on the land, he seemed out of place working in a chemical plant. Due to his short sightedness, he wore glasses with thick lenses and the prescription appeared not to suit him, because he would tilt his head back and look down through them when he spoke to anyone. He was also partially deaf as a result of a rather stupid accident with his old Morris Minor car. When driving to a shoot, his dog would travel on the front seat beside him with the gun upright between them. With his poor eyesight it is difficult to understand why he went shooting because the wildlife would be in no danger, which is more than can be said of anyone near him. On this occasion he had left the gun loaded with the safety catch off. When he braked suddenly, the dog was thrown forward hitting the trigger with its paw and the explosion blew a hole in the fabric sunroof of the car. Although both escaped injury, his hearing and presumably the dog, never fully recovered.

As a manager, I occasionally needed to interview people to fill vacancies in the plant. In the first instance an applicant would be interviewed by the Personnel Department before being passed on to me for approval. The name "Personnel Department" has nowadays been replaced by the rather pretentious, self-inflating title of "Human Resources" or "HR" as they more often like to be called. Do they not realise that they deal with real people who are like them and not to be classed in the same manner as material resources?

Keith was our Personnel Manager, a likeable fellow in charge of an office staffed by real people who were just as human and fallible as the rest of us normal folk. On one occasion they sent me a man for interview who appeared to have a speech impediment until, halfway through our conversation, he fell off his chair and had to be helped to his feet. When I finally saw him off the site I phoned Personnel and said, "Keith, the man you just sent to me was pissed out of his head", to which he replied, "I know Ron – but I wanted to see what you thought of him!"

Also memorable was the case of a very suitable chap who I accepted for a job which entailed mixing chemicals by tipping the contents of fairly heavy sacks into vats of water in an area where the floor was always wet. After a couple of weeks he asked for a day off to attend hospital to have his leg seen to. It was then I was shocked to learn that he had a false leg, which needed regular adjustment. When he left my office I phoned Keith to complain that he'd sent me a man with only one leg to lift weights on a slippery floor. His rather surprising reply was, "Well Ron, you interviewed him!" With a note of sarcasm I said, "So sorry Keith – my mistake – I forgot to ask him how many legs he had." With a bit of reorganisation we managed to find him a more suitable job.

10

Ice Plant

Sedum spectabile

The 1980s of Margaret Thatcher's government were marked by nationwide recession and its chill effects were felt across the whole spectrum of manufacturing, including the chemical industry. In the case of my own company, the shrinking business meant that its only hope of survival was to downsize and move to a smaller site in the northwest where development grants were available to provide employment in areas where the recession had hit hardest.

There were therefore two options open to me, either to relocate with them – a risky move in a shrinking business and a poor economic climate – or to accept a reasonably generous redundancy settlement. In the event I chose the second course, which was perhaps just as risky, although it presented an exciting new challenge. In many ways it may have been a foolhardy move because my daughter Nicky was very young and the interest rates on the mortgage repayments had soared alarmingly, as indeed had the local council tax.

Since I had some years experience as a keen amateur

gardener, I thought it would be a good idea to start up a small horticultural business offering landscaping and maintenance work. It also offered the opportunity to study the subject formally at the local agricultural college, so I enrolled for a two-year course on the basis of one day per week. A large part of the syllabus dealt with horticultural machinery, and apart from providing an essential breakdown service, it was also invaluable for solving any problems encountered in the course of my work.

My first idea was to offer a landscaping service for factories. Having spent many years in industry, I knew that most factory sites were an untidy mess and could be improved with staff amenity areas for alfresco eating as well as planting both outside and in reception and office areas.

After distributing my first leaflets, I realised that I hadn't really thought it through, because the recession was the very reason I was offering the service in the first place and the last thing a struggling firm would do was spend money on improving its site. After having a zero response, I then circulated leaflets to all businesses within a ten-mile radius and this finally produced a couple of results.

One of these was a down-at-heel large hotel that was being redeveloped by a major brewery as a motel. The brief was to maintain the fairly extensive grounds, with payment deferred until they were ready for trading eight weeks later.

After a couple of weeks, I was asked to attend a site meeting with the management and architects from the brewery to discuss some landscaping improvement projects on the site. Although this initially had to be funded from my dwindling redundancy settlement, it proved to be a lucky break and at further site meetings the architects showed me plans and asked me to tender for three other sites. I was naturally delighted to be given such a volume of business, but there are, of course, many risks in having too much work too soon for a small organisation and over-trading has been the cause of collapse of many successful businesses.

One of my most challenging projects was to landscape a large neglected garden at the rear of a pub that was being modernised. Most of the area was to be levelled and laid to lawn with nearly two thousand turfs. Due to the building work running late, we were unable to start work until late on the Friday night and the grand reopening was to take place at 7pm on the Monday. Working in the dark we managed to clear the site of brushwood and builder's rubble in time to start rotavating and levelling on the Saturday and Sunday to be ready for delivery of the turf and plants on Monday morning. To add to our difficulties we were in the middle of a heat wave and we had to lay the turf under sprinklers while wearing swimming trunks. The job was finally completed while the dignitaries were making the opening speeches. Although it is customary to allow turf to settle for about two weeks, in this case the staff were putting out the picnic tables and the lawn was soon filled with people for the rest of the evening. I have subsequently visited the pub and the lawn is in quite good condition, so I suppose some rules are meant to be broken.

Another interesting project was to prepare beds and

plant shrubs in the car park of a well-known pub that was also undergoing renovation in London's east end.

The site manager was an outspoken friendly fellow who was dressed and spoke rather like a market trader. He greeted me warmly and said he was under some pressure to complete the job. I asked him if he had any preferences for the type of shrubs to be planted, to which he replied "Forns Ron." I then started to describe the various types of thorn-bearing shrubs and asked what he thought might be suitable, to which his reply was "Big buggers. Anyfink else and the bastards'll nick 'em!" As far as I'm aware the 'forns' are still there.

With payments now coming in at random intervals, I was walking a tightrope having to fund materials and the casual labour of fellow students. I was well aware that the risk could be smoothed over with bank loans but I have an inherent mistrust of bankers. I have known quite a few business colleagues who were driven to the wall after being refused credit by them as soon as a small dip occurred in an otherwise successful business. I simply fail to understand how people who handle so much money can show such a lack of basic business sense and be driven by greed to seek high returns from foolhardy ventures. I'm firmly of the opinion that all trainee bank employees should be made to spend at least a couple of months running a small business to gain experience of the real world.

As events turned out, I managed my balancing act successfully and was able to put two fingers up to the banks and even managed to build up a reasonable reserve to fund future jobs.

Things were also starting to develop with domestic work, as I began to gain a reputation for garden design and landscaping at fair rates, which I was able to offer as a result of low overheads. I was also lucky enough to be able to employ keen students from my contacts at college. Although hard working and doubtless knowledgeable in matters horticultural, some of them seemed to have a distant spaced-out demeanour that may have been attributable to sampling the leaves of some of the exotic plants in the college glasshouses.

With the increasing volume of work I now found it necessary to employ the odd full-time trainee and these proved to be of variable capability. One of my star trainees was an attractive young girl who was a very hard worker. Her speech, however, belied her appearance and on one occasion I had left some piles of well-rotted farmyard manure for her to apply as a mulch to a shrub border, after she had tidied up the plants. It was a rather formal hotel with many elderly upper-class guests, who were dining out on the lawn on a fine warm day. As I was on the other side of the lawn her loud penetrating voice yelled across to me "RON – WHAT DO I DO WITH ALL THIS SHIT?" I think most of the people found it amusing whilst revelling in my embarrassment. Most of my trainees stayed with me for several months so I think they enjoyed the experience.

Frank was a middle-aged man who had spent almost all his working life in the building trade and joined me on a landscape project, after he had been laid off. I found his experience particularly useful for those paving and construction jobs that I must admit are not my forte. Robert was one of my trainees on the same project – a rather gullible young lad who was a natural target for Frank's dry sense of humour. With a serious deadpan expression he would hold Robert's attention while stringing him along with the most ridiculous stories. On one occasion I heard him telling Robert that he used to have a crease mark down each cheek where his mother would breast-feed him through the school railings. On another, Frank told him he was particularly well endowed because his mum only had one arm and used to lift him out of the bath with it! The best part was Robert's look of total belief while Frank showed no trace of a smile. I was sorry when he left me near the end of the project, but he found work on a large building site that seemed to offer more permanence.

John had recently moved into a semi-detatched bungalow in our neighbourhood, after spending most of his life in the heart of the Oxfordshire countryside, living in a small thatched farm cottage. As he had now retired, I think his cottage may have been needed for another farm worker, but it also suited his purpose to move to a less rural location. He quickly became well known locally as a friendly, outgoing character who would easily engage total strangers in deep conversation.

Occasionally, when I was pressed for another pair of hands, he readily offered to help out and would try to shun any offer of payment. Having spent a lifetime working with soil he was a good worker who enjoyed getting his hands dirty again.

Typical of most rural folk, he attended the local church service every Sunday evening, almost as a way of life rather than from a deep religious conviction although, of course, he had his own firm beliefs. After repeatedly asking me to go with him, I did give in on one occasion, just to keep him quiet.

We took our place together near the back of the church, almost empty except for a few of the devout faithful regulars near the front. As he gazed around at the mass of empty pews he gave me a nudge and whispered, "What we need, Ron, is another war. That'll get the buggers on their knees." Because our experiences of the last war were totally different, with him being tucked away in the depths of Oxfordshire, I had some reservations with his sentiments, but I had to admit he did have a point. Sadly, he died after a fairly short and severe illness, but he did at least fully enjoy his brief retirement.

As a newcomer to landscaping, I was often offered projects that I felt were well beyond my capability, even with the safety net provided by the college. When I started the business however, I made a firm resolve that I would never turn away a challenge and business opportunity. I realise that clients are not interested in doubts and problems associated with the job. The bottom line is simply that it can be done and the price. As Dad would say, "A man who never made a mistake never made anything." Although I always made a thorough survey, on a couple of occasions hidden problems went undetected, which fortunately didn't incur losses, but lowered my profit from the job. I have known instances where unforeseen problems have been the ruin of small businesses. Fortunately, in most cases my estimates would be accepted because other clients had recommended me. It was also surprising that many problems that at first worried me, proved to be easier as the work progressed and the end result gave me a pleasant feeling of self-satisfaction. The additional bonus was that I was gaining valuable experience to tackle bigger projects and many of my clients have now become firm friends.

Inevitably, a point comes in all businesses when a choice has to be made between developing the business further in response to increasing trade, or to turn work down and stay small. In the event I was not prepared to take the risk of overtrading and decided on the latter course where I was earning a comfortable living. Perhaps if I had been younger things may have turned out somewhat differently.

Another stroke of good fortune occurred when I was asked to lecture in horticulture at another college. These were so successful that I was asked to start a full-time horticulture course on a one-day-per-week basis. This is an aspect of my career that I thoroughly enjoyed as I found a great sense of self-fulfilment in finding that other people benefited from my experience. As things developed further I found I was lecturing at two colleges with an evening City & Guilds gardening class at a third. Furthermore, I even found I had a talent for teaching mathematics. As I grew older and found I was unable to cope with some of the harder tasks of landscaping, I found that teaching gradually replaced the more strenuous aspects of the business and has now provided a satisfying career to carry on into retirement.

Sadly, I lost Joan in 2008 after a long and unequal

fight with emphysema caused by her history of smoking, and I have found working to be a great comfort. Needless to say there is always a penalty to be paid for doing lighter physical work and this manifests itself in a tendency to obesity and a loss of condition as the body reacts to unaccustomed lack of use. I'm blessed, however, by the presence of Nicky and her husband Steve who live nearby with their young twins Hannah and Owen. Their seemingly constant domestic crises still exercise my DIY skills to the full, so relaxation is not an option.

So far, I have managed to avoid the question of when I will eventually retire, but if I were pushed for an answer it would simply be, "I won't"!

Finally, to end on a floral note, I feel I should devote some space to my favourite flower, the Madonna Lily – *Lilium candidum* – perhaps inspired by the following text from the New Testament:

> *Consider the lilies of the field how they grow. They toil not neither do they spin, yet Solomon in all his glory was never arrayed like one of these.*
>
> Matthew 6:28

Every June I look forward to its arrival to be delighted by the sheer beauty of its dazzling white, waxy petals forming the trumpet and the glistening opalescence of the inner surface. The large male stamens surrounding the central stigma are overloaded with the most brilliant orange-yellow pollen and, in addition, Nature has bestowed on it the most delicious heady perfume.

As a horticulturist, I agree that this is simply a product of evolution, but the nuts and bolts of genetics fall far short of explaining the mysteries and secrets of life itself that lie hidden in such a simple flower and will never be revealed to us. Even more wondrous is the fact that, in many different forms, this is replicated countless millions of times in the grasses and wildflowers of our fields and meadows. Often too tiny and complex to be appreciated by our dull senses, they are carelessly trodden under without our even being aware of the beauty that lies beneath our feet. My final quotation therefore, is attributed to that fine poet, William Butler Yeats, who wrote:

"Tread softly, for you tread on my dreams."